Ripley's

Believe It or Not!®

Ripley's Believe It or Not!

ARTS & ENTERTAINMENT

RIPLEY PUBLISHING

a Jim Pattison Company

Developed and produced
by Miles Kelly Publishing

Publishing Director   Anne Marshall
Senior Editor   Jenni Rainford
Assistant Editor   Teri Mort
Designers   John Christopher, Jo Brewer
Picture Research   Liberty Newton
Copy Editor   Rosalind Beckman
Sub Editor   Jim Murphy
Text   Clive Carpenter, Windsor Chorlton,
                           Peter Eldin, John Farndon, Geoff Tibballs
Indexer   Lynda Watson
Production Manager   Estela Boulton
Jacket Design   Tony Collins
Color Separation   DPI Colour Digital Ltd, Essex, U.K.

ISBN 10: 1-893951-15-4
ISBN 13: 978-1-893951-15-0

1 3 5 7 9 10 8 6 4 2

Printed in China

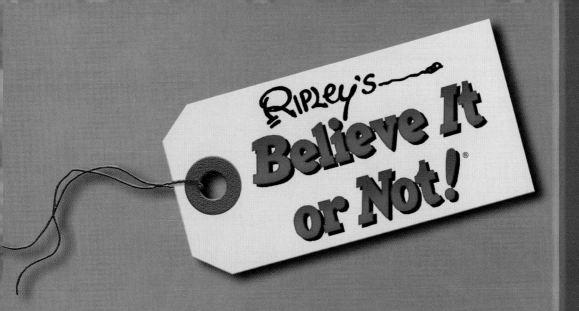

CONTENTS

Arts & Entertainment

is a collection of extraordinary accounts of

artistic oddities. Read about a statue of King Kong

made from popcorn, the man with the xylophone

head, and the guy who ate a small airplane

—all in this breathtaking book.

◀ Musicians play their instruments at an
underwater music festival in Florida...

Butter Sculptor

The *Last Supper* carved entirely from butter was sculpted by 74-year-old Norma Lyon of Des Moines, Iowa, in 1999, working in her cooler at 42°F (5°C).

For over 40 years Norma has sculpted a life-sized cow for the Iowa State Fair using 600 lb (272 kg) of butter. Using a wood, wire, metal, and steel mesh frame she softens buckets of five-year-old butter outside the cooler before moving into the cold and applying layers until a cow emerges, measuring 5.5 ft (0.2 m) high and 8 ft (2.5 m) long. After leaving the cow to set for 20 to 30 minutes she finely sculpts the head and the body, working down the legs to the hooves—24 hours of butter sculpture! Norma's work includes a Harley-Davidson motorcycle, and a life-size sculpture of John Wayne.

ARTY FACTS

- Van Gogh only sold one painting in his entire lifetime—*Red Vineyard at Arles*
- Jean Dakessian, an artist in California, painted 50 oil pumps to look like insects and animals
- Salvador Dali once held a party at which every guest came dressed as a bad dream
- Paul Gauguin worked on the building of the Panama Canal

Norma Lyon's biggest project yet, The Last Supper sculpted from a staggering 1,800 lb (815 kg) of butter in 1999.

Brush Stroke

Arriving for work in October 2001, Emmanuel Asare, a cleaner at a fashionable art gallery in London, Eyestorm, found that the room had been left in a complete mess following an exhibition party. Empty beer bottles, paint-covered newspapers, and candy wrappings were strewn all over the place. So he diligently set to work sweeping up the bits and pieces and dumping them in garbage bags. Next day he reported for duty, only to be told by gallery bosses: "That was no rubbish you cleared—that was a £5,000 ($8,000) work of art by the great Damien Hirst!"

Day Job Dutch master Vincent van Gogh (1853–90) painted one picture each day for the last 70 days of his life.

Night Shift French artist Anne-Louis Girodet (1767–1824) found that he worked better at night. So that he could see in the dark, he would light up to 40 candles around the brim of his hat, later calculating his fee according to the number of candles burned while he painted the picture.

DIFFERENT HANDLES

When French artist Louis François Roubillac (1705–62) started work on his sculpture of composer George Friedrich Handel he decided he didn't like Handel's ears. So he modelled the ears of a London lady instead.

Made from Scratch Californian artist Tim Hawkinson likes to model sculptures from parts of his body. His favorite work of art is a 2-in (5-cm) tall piece called *Bird* that was made entirely from his fingernails!

Foot Prints Upside-down Kansas City artist, Jimmie McPherson, was able to draw pictures with both his feet at the same time.

Food Drawer Michelangelo (1475–1564) created a still-life drawing of wine, fruit, bread, and spaghetti as a shopping list left for his cook who was unable to read.

Smile in the Mirror Leonardo da Vinci's famous painting *The Mona Lisa* was originally bought by King Francis I of France to hang in his bathroom.

Winner's Cup American sculptor Tom Friedman pinned a Styrofoam cup with coffee stains to a piece of wood, added a ladybug, and called it *Untitled*. In 2001 it sold at auction for $30,000 (£18,000).

Waste Disposal Drivers using the Eastshore Freeway at Emeryville, California, in 1987 were amazed to see over 100 driftwood sculptures spread out along a mile of roadside. The eye-catching sculptures, which included a train, were created from waste material carried in by the tide.

In 2003, students from London's Camberwell College of Arts spent 630 hours creating the world's biggest popcorn sculpture—a 13 ft (4 m) statue of King Kong, weighing 1,720 lb (800 kg)— that's as much as four gorillas!

Bumper Crop Jon Bedford, an artist from Santa Fe, New Mexico, has created amazing sculptures out of chrome car bumpers! He transforms the scrap metal into birds and animals, including a life-size rhinoceros!

BAGS OF TALENT

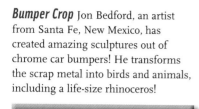

Using ordinary brown paper grocery bags, Anton Schiavone, an artist from Bangor, Pennsylvania, created magnificent life-size replicas of the masters, including Leonardo da Vinci's *The Last Supper* and Michelangelo's *La Pieta*.

The brown paper bag replica of Michelangelo's La Pieta by Anton Schiavone.

Desk Work Yugoslav performance artist Marina Abramovic spent 12 days on three raised desks at a New York City gallery in November 2002. Existing solely on water, she lived in full public view for the entire time. She said the idea of the performance was to heighten her senses and transmit energy to her audience.

Eye Liner Visual artist Jochem Hendricks of Frankfurt, Germany, creates works of art by drawing with his eyes instead of his hands. He uses an eyescanner that converts data to actual lines.

Motor Mountain Located in Jouy-en-Josas, France, the 65-ft (20-m) high sculpture *Long-Term Parking* by Arman comprises 60 cars embedded in 1,600 tons of concrete.

Angry because his art was unknown in Rome, Italian painter Salvator Rosa (1615–73) disguised himself as "Dr Formica" and prescribed "the art of Salvator Rosa" as a cure for mental depression. Rosa's ruse worked and he soon became one of the city's most famous artists.

Capsized In 1961 the Museum of Modern Art in New York proudly displayed *Le Bateau*, a painting by celebrated French artist Henri Matisse. It took seven weeks before someone spotted that it had been hung upside-down.

Soft Approach In 1999 Indian sculptor Anant Narayan Khairnar finished a 7-ft (2-m) tall statue of Mahatma Gandhi—made entirely from cotton! It took him 11 months to complete the sculpture.

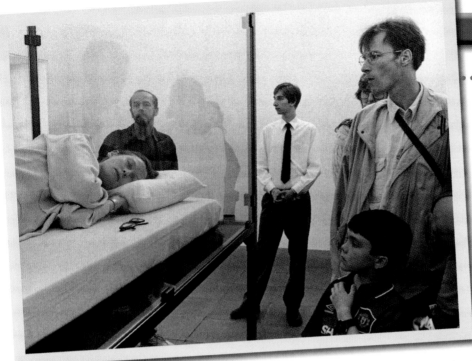

In 1995 London's Serpentine Gallery showed The Maybe, an exhibit by Tilda Swinton, which consisted solely of her sleeping on a mattress on a shelf in the center of a room for eight hours a day.

Barred When French artist Cézanne applied to enter the École des Beaux-Arts, he was turned down!

True Grit French painter Sarah Biffin was born without limbs. She was able to paint by clasping the paintbrush or pencil tightly between her teeth.

Snappy Gift American artist Charles Willson Peale, not only painted George Washington but presented him with a set of dentures made from elks' teeth!

Moving Exhibits The Andy Warhol Museum located in Pittsburg, exhibits unusual art and sculpture as well as playing host to Tibetan monk dance routines.

Sole Survivor The murals in the court of the Algerian Palace of Hadj-Ahmed Constantine were painted in the 19th-century by a shoemaker. Hadj-Ahmed thought all Frenchmen were artists so he ordered a captive French shoemaker to decorate the palace wall or suffer death.

Sinking Funds *Drains*, a sculpture of a sink stopper by U.S. artist Robert Gober, sold for over $55,000 (£32,000) in 1995. Gober said the work represented "a window onto another world."

Ape Fan Congo, a chimpanzee at the London Zoo in the 1950s, was such a talented artist that the great Pablo Picasso bought one of his paintings.

Lick of Paint Huang Erh-nan, a Chinese artist of the 1920s, did not paint with a brush. Instead he used his tongue.

WATERED COLORS

An accident in 1983 left Belgian scuba diver Jamy Verheylewegen crippled for 18 months. During this time, he produced more than 400 paintings underwater, using oil paints on synthetic fiber. His boards were mounted on an easel that was weighed down with lead.

He Gave His All

Thinking he was dying from tuberculosis, Japanese sculptor Hananuma Masakichi wanted to leave a gift to the woman he loved. So, working with adjustable mirrors, he used around 2,000 pieces of wood to carve a full-size image of himself. He plucked out his own nails, teeth, and hair to finish the work. He later recovered and, having lost these vital parts, also lost his girlfriend!

Ripley's ®
MASAKICHI WOOD MODEL
EXHIBIT NO: 12983
CARVED IN THE 1890S AS A SELF-PORTRAIT FOR THE GIRLFRIEND MASAKICHI THOUGHT HE WOULD LEAVE BEHIND

Toast of Japan

Japanese artist Tadahiko Ogawa has used slices of toasted bread to recreate such famous works of art as Da Vinci's *Mona Lisa* and Michelangelo's *Creation.*

Ogawa draws his pictures, traces them on to aluminum foil, and then cuts the foil into toaster-size pieces. He wraps the foil around the bread and cuts the foil away from the areas he wants to brown (toast). Each piece of bread is individually toasted to the desired color— lightly toasted to burned! The toast is then put together as a mosaic to create the final work. Ogawa has completed about 50 old masters including Da Vinci's *The Last Supper* and Botticelli's *Birth of Venus.*

Mona Lisa *made from 63 pieces of toast— lightly toasted to burned!*

Ripley's—— ®

CREATION
EXHIBIT NO: 13843
OGAWA'S "CREATION" IS MADE
ENTIRELY FROM PIECES OF TOAST

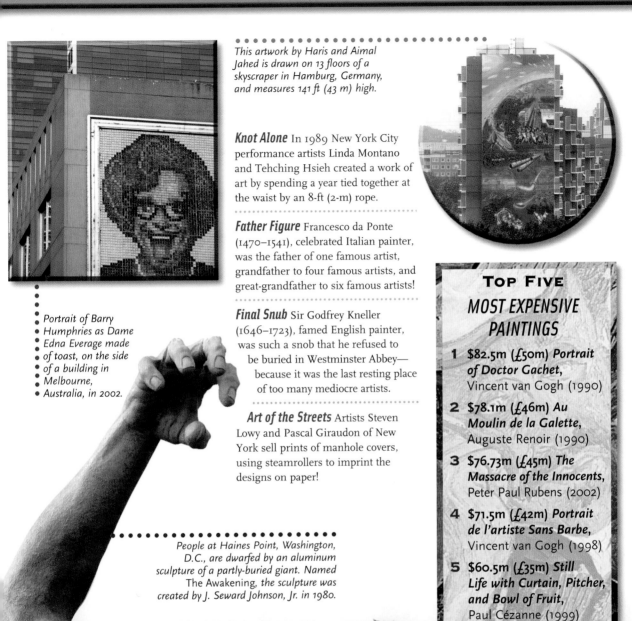

This artwork by Haris and Aimal Jahed is drawn on 13 floors of a skyscraper in Hamburg, Germany, and measures 141 ft (43 m) high.

Knot Alone In 1989 New York City performance artists Linda Montano and Tehching Hsieh created a work of art by spending a year tied together at the waist by an 8-ft (2-m) rope.

Father Figure Francesco da Ponte (1470–1541), celebrated Italian painter, was the father of one famous artist, grandfather to four famous artists, and great-grandfather to six famous artists!

Final Snub Sir Godfrey Kneller (1646–1723), famed English painter, was such a snob that he refused to be buried in Westminster Abbey—because it was the last resting place of too many mediocre artists.

Art of the Streets Artists Steven Lowy and Pascal Giraudon of New York sell prints of manhole covers, using steamrollers to imprint the designs on paper!

Portrait of Barry Humphries as Dame Edna Everage made of toast, on the side of a building in Melbourne, Australia, in 2002.

People at Haines Point, Washington, D.C., are dwarfed by an aluminum sculpture of a partly-buried giant. Named The Awakening, the sculpture was created by J. Seward Johnson, Jr. in 1980.

TOP FIVE
MOST EXPENSIVE PAINTINGS

1 $82.5m (£50m) *Portrait of Doctor Gachet*, Vincent van Gogh (1990)

2 $78.1m (£46m) *Au Moulin de la Galette*, Auguste Renoir (1990)

3 $76.73m (£45m) *The Massacre of the Innocents*, Peter Paul Rubens (2002)

4 $71.5m (£42m) *Portrait de l'artiste Sans Barbe*, Vincent van Gogh (1998)

5 $60.5m (£35m) *Still Life with Curtain, Pitcher, and Bowl of Fruit*, Paul Cézanne (1999)

Cents of History Art Grant of San Francisco, California, created a two-dimensional sculpture of a stagecoach using one million pennies.

PAINTINGS THAT REALLY LIVE!
An exhibition at Soho's New Museum of Contemporary Art in New York City in 1988 offered visitors the unique experience of shaking hands with "paintings," featuring artists actually standing inside large frames on the walls for up to 7 hours!

Speed Worker Denny Dent, a U.S. artist pays tribute to musical artists by painting a portrait of them faster than the time it takes to play one of their songs!

"Cadillac Ranch" livens up historic Route 66 in Texas. A collection of artists known as "Ant Farm" created the flamboyant sculpture as a tribute to America's favorite mode of transportation.

Art House A painting by Albert Bierstadt, a 19th-century landscape artist, measured over 150 sq ft (14 sq m) and was so large that a house had to be built around it!

Don't Get Up British artist Tracey Emin created a work of art that consisted of her old unmade bed—complete with dirty sheets, an empty vodka bottle, and old tissues. It was sold for $225,000!

Dotty Driver Artist Tyree Guyton has decorated his car in Detroit, Michigan, with thousands of polka dots.

Ripley's ®
JELLYBEAN ROULETTE WHEEL
EXHIBIT NO: 13154
THIS ROULETTE WHEEL IS MADE FROM
14,000 JELLYBEANS, IN 25 DIFFERENT
COLORS, WEIGHING 80 LB (36 KG)

Artist Peter Rocha has also made jellybean portraits, including one of former president, Ronald Reagan.

Public Autopsy!

Nearly 50 people paid about $20 dollars each for ringside seats to watch the public dissection of a 72-year-old deceased German businessman in England in 2002. This ambitious artistic performance by Professor Gunther von Hagens was Britain's first public autopsy in over a century.

German pathologist, Gunther von Hagens has developed a technique of plastination—impregnating human organs and entire corpses with liquid plastic to stop the body from decomposing. His 2002 show "Body Worlds," featured 25 skinned human corpses. He has also worked with horses, including one exhibit that showed a mounted rider whose outstretched arm holds his own brain.

Von Hagens styled himself on the doctor in Rembrandt's painting, The Anatomy Lesson of Dr. Nicolaes Tulp, *by wearing a black fedora (hat) and a surgical gown. The autopsy of this 72-year-old man was broadcast on British television.*

The Basketball Player *created by Gunther von Hagens, using a real body.*

In 1991 British artist Marc Quinn produced Self, *a sculptural self-portrait of his head made from nine pints of his own blood donated over a period of five months.*

BLIND ARTIST PAINTS WITH FEELING

British artist Gary Sargeant lost his sight—but still manages to paint. He visits the scene of the picture and with the help of his wife measures dimensions, either with his blind stick that is marked in finger-length notches and walking out distances between objects, or feeling textures by touch. By measuring and using masking tape, he builds up the canvas and then starts work. As the paint builds up he "reads" it, and from his many years of experience painting as a sighted person interprets what the picture should look like.

Long Hall The Louvre Museum in Paris, home to Leonardo da Vinci's *Mona Lisa*, has an exterior that is 2.5 mi (4 km) in length!

Lookalikes Patience Lovell Wright (1725–86) created life-size wax models of famous English royalty and politicians. She was the first recorded sculptor in the American colonies.

Final Move Though French Cubist Marcel Duchamp embraced sculpture in favor of painting, he later embraced chess in favor of sculpture!

Slow Starter When Pablo Picasso was born, he was left for dead by a midwife who believed him to be stillborn. However, a nearby relative quickly spotted the baby was alive and came to the rescue by reviving him!

Massive Collection The Hermitage and Winter Palace in St. Petersburg, Russia, is home to almost three million works of art. The palace itself has an amazing 1,786 doors, 1,945 windows and over 1,000 rooms!

"Asian Field," an exhibit by English artist Antony Gormley, in Beijing in 2003, is made from 192,000 clay figures—each one no bigger than your hand!

A Head for Writing

Tapan Dey can write with a pen clipped to his hair or with one protruding from his mouth, a nostril or even an ear!

Indian street performer Dey from Basirhat, West Bengal, must be the world's most unconventional writer. Even when he uses his hands, he still insists on doing things differently—and writes with all four limbs at the same time by inserting pens between his fingers and toes! The 27-year-old can also write amazingly well in four different languages—Hindi, Assamese, English, and Bangla. Dey, who wants to redefine the art of calligraphy, says: "I was inspired when I saw a young boy in Calcutta writing with both hands. I thought I could do better."

Tapan Dey puts pen to paper using a pen that is pinned on to his hair!

From Russia With . . . Suspicion Karl Marx once wrote to his friend, Friedrich Engels, expressing his distrust of the entire Russian population!

BOOK BAN

- *Little Red Riding Hood,* folktale—U.S.A., alcoholism
- *Huckleberry Finn,* Mark Twain—U.S.A., racism
- *The Adventures of Sherlock Holmes,* Sir Arthur Conan Doyle—U.S.S.R., occultism
- *Frankenstein,* Mary Shelley —South Africa, indecency
- *The Merchant of Venice,* William Shakespeare— U.S.A., offensive to Jews

Start to Finish English writer Mary Shelley (1797–1851) wrote *Frankenstein* when she was just 19. By contrast, Alice Pollock of Haslemere, England, had her first book, *Portrait of My Victorian Youth,* published when she was 102.

True North English novelist Charles Dickens (1812–70) thought his writing would improve if he slept facing north! He always carried a compass with him to check his direction.

Sights Unseen Even though he was totally blind and journeyed without a companion, British writer James Holman (1786–1857) wrote a number of excellent travel books graphically describing his adventures in many lands.

The strangest library in all history! Saheb Ibn Abad (938–995), the Grand Vizier of Persia, always traveled with 117,000 books— even when he went to war. His mobile library was carried on 400 camels, which were trained to walk in alphabetical order so any book could be located immediately.

Grain of Truth

The 65 words, 254 letters of the Lord's Prayer inscribed on one single grain of rice! Rice writers were employed at the Ripley's odditoriums in the 1930s to produce grains to sell as souvenirs. This piece is thought to have been done by E.L. ("The Amazing") Blystone of Ardara, Pennsylvania—he used no form of magnification to work and his personal record was an amazing 1615 letters on a single grain!

The Lord's Prayer written on a single grain of rice.

Multi-tasking French painter Claude Monet (1840–1926) often worked on as many as six paintings at the same time!

BOUND WITH HUMAN SKIN

After John Horwood was hanged in 1821, when he was found guilty of murder, his body was given to Bristol Royal Infirmary in England for dissection. The anatomist, Richard Smith, published his findings in a book and paid a local tanner to turn the murderer's flayed skin into leather with which to bind the tome together. The book went on public display for the first time in 2003.

Slow Reader In 1650 the Bishop of Winchester, England, borrowed a book from Somerset County Records Office. It was eventually returned to Somerset County Library in 1985, having built up a fine of £3,000 ($5,000). Its title? *The Book of Fines.*

Fueled by Coffee The French writer Voltaire (1694–1778) drank an average of 70 cups of coffee a day!

A banana mailed to a Connecticut hospital with two postage stamps in 1988 arrived safely! The address for Rachela Colonna and the message—"I love you" in Italian—were written on the peel and the stamps were covered with clear tape.

A woman who bought a hardback version of the then unknown Harry Potter and the Sorcerer's Stone for £10.99 ($18) in 1997 sold it for £13,000 ($21,600) at auction in 2002. Amazingly successful, Harry Potter (Daniel Radcliffe) is seen here in Harry Potter and the Chamber of Secrets (U.S. 2002) with Ron Weasley (Rupert Grint).

Potter Mania A 93-word "teaser card" written by J.K. Rowling and holding clues to the plot of *Harry Potter and the Order of the Phoenix* was sold to a private U.S. collector six months before publication of the novel—for $46,600 (£28,680)!

Think Ink Denied the use of pen or pencil, René Auguste de Renneville (1650–1723), a prisoner in the Bastille for 11 years, wrote 6,000 lines of romantic poetry and a ten-volume history book using split chicken bones dipped in a mixture of soot and wine.

Flexible Letters The 26 letters of the English alphabet can be made into 403,290,000,000,000,000,000,000,000 different combinations.

ALPHA BITS

• The Cambodian alphabet has 74 letters, while the Rotokas in Papua New Guinea has just 11 letters—a, b, e, g, i, k, o, p, r, t, and u.

• The only 15-letter word that can be spelled without repeating a letter is "uncopyrightable."

• If you were to spell out numbers, you would have to go to "one thousand" before you found the letter "a."

• There is no single word to say "yes" or "no" in Japanese.

• The only ten-letter word you can spell using just the top row of letters of a keyboard is "typewriter."

Dorothy Nusbaum of Washington, D.C. was ambidexterous and could write two different sentences simultaneously. She could also write backward with her left hand!

Tintype Laurent de la Baumille, 18th-century poet and playwright, while held as a prisoner in the Bastille in 1752, wrote a tragedy by scratching the words onto two tin plates with a needle! Although the plates were confiscated, he had memorized the words and the play was later performed in French theaters.

Italian poet Alighieri Dante (1265–1321) had a phobia about candlesticks. So he trained a cat to hold a lighted candle in its paws while he wrote.

Frontier Library The front door of the Haskell Free Library and Opera House at Derby Line, Vermont, is in the U.S.A. But the back door is in Quebec province, Canada. During World War II, Canadian visitors to the front door had to show their passports.

Favorite Tale Countess Yekaterina Skavronskaya (1761–1829) of Russia enjoyed the same story 24,090 times! She was lulled to sleep by the same fairy tale told by the same servant every night for 66 years—until the day she died.

Book behind Bars The last prisoner in the Bastille was a book! By order of King Louis XVI, the *Dictionnaire Encyclopédique* was sentenced to life imprisonment for the crimes of liberalism and disloyalty to the state.

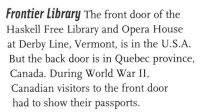

POET'S CRUMBS

In 1857, Alfred, Lord Tennyson, Queen Victoria's Poet Laureate, earned less than her official rat-catcher!

Career in Shreds After laboring for 13 years writing a book about Swedish economic solutions, business consultant Ulf af Trolle finally took his 250-page manuscript to be copied. Yet it took just seconds for his life's work to be reduced to 50,000 strips of paper when a worker confused the copier with the shredder!

WORD WISE

• *Gone With The Wind* was Margaret Mitchell's only book

• The Bible is the most shop-lifted book in the U.S.A

• The first book on plastic surgery was written in 1597

Flock of Poems

English writer Valerie Laws spray-painted words from a poem onto a flock of sheep in 2002 to see whether the animals would then arrange themselves to form a new poem as they wandered about the field. Northern Arts awarded her a grant of $3,400 (£2,000) for the project, which, she said, would be an exercise in both "random" literature and quantum mechanics.

One of the poems created by Valerie Laws' experiment read: "Warm, Drift, Graze, Gentle, White below the sky. Soft, Sheep, Mirrors, Snow, Clouds.

Uphill The Maori name for a particular hill on New Zealand's North Island runs to a staggering 85 letters—taumatawhakatangihangakoauauotamateaturipukakapikimaungahoronukupokaiwhenuakitanatahu. Translated into English, this name means "The place where Tamatea, the man with the big knees, who slid, climbed, and swallowed mountains, known as landeater, played his flute to his loved one."

Times of Plenty One issue of the *New York Times* contains more information than the average person in the 16th century would have read throughout their entire life.

Undaunted Author John Creasy, a British author, received a total of 774 rejection slips before finally getting his 564 books published.

BEVELIE It or Not!
Apratneply it dsoen't mtaetr waht oderr the ltetres in a word are, the olny ipmoratnt tihng is taht the fisrt and lsat ltetre be in the rhgit palce. The rset can be a toatl mses and you can stlil raed it whituot a porbelm. Tihs is bacesue the hamun mnid deos not raed evrey ltetre by itlesf, but the wrod as a wolhe.

Miniature copies of the Koran (top), Hindu holy book the Bhagavad-Gita (middle) and the Holy Bible (bottom).

TEMPTING TITLES

- *A Pictorial Book of Tongue Coating*
- *Amputation Stumps: Their Care and After-treatment*
- *Holiday Retreats for Cats and Dogs in England*
- *All About Mud*
- *Canadian National Egg Laying Contests*

Do it Yourself George Bernard Shaw created a new way for spelling fish: "Ghoti" to highlight inconsistencies in pronunciation of certain letters. "Gh as in "enough", "o" as in "women," and "ti" as in "nation."

Arab Influence Many words we use daily are derived from Arabic words such as "algebra," "average," and "tabby." Algebra means a reunion of broken parts; average means damaged goods; tabby means a cloth with stripes.

Heavy Going The Arabic *Legislations Encyclopedia* is so massive it weighs a staggering 925 lb (420 kg) and has an index that takes up six volumes!

A Key Change The first typed manuscript was submitted to a publisher by author Mark Twain.

Thriller Bee Show

Dr. Norman Gary, professor of entomology at the University of California, tours the world with his Thriller Bee Show, playing Dixieland jazz on the clarinet while as many as 100,000 bees swarm all over him and often even enter his mouth!

Apart from a passion for bees, 60-year-old Dr. Norman Gary plays the clarinet (in bee flat!) in a band called The Beez Kneez.

During each performance, which take place inside a plexiglass cage to prevent the bees from escaping, scores of bees will enter his mouth and buzz around inside. A few sting him every time, but their stings don't bother him. Dr. Gary, a self-styled bee psychologist who has studied honeybees for more than 30 years, has written around 100 scientific papers on the insects' behavior.

TOP FIVE
MOST PLAYED SONGS

20th century favorites on U.S. radio and TV

1 **"You've Lost That Lovin' Feelin,"** The Righteous Brothers

2 **"Never My Love,"** The Association

3 **"Yesterday,"** The Beatles

4 **"Stand By Me,"** Ben E. King

5 **"Can't Take My Eyes Off You,"** Andy Williams

Blowing Bubbles

The world's most unusual music venue is situated 30 ft (9 m) beneath the surface of the sea off the coast of Florida. In July 2003 nearly 400 people dived below the waves to hear the 19th annual Lower Keys Underwater Music Festival.

QUIRKY NOTES

- Beethoven poured jugs of iced water over his head to help creativity
- A violin contains some 70 separate pieces of wood
- Replica kettle drums were once used as currency in Indonesia
- There are over 50,000 official Elvis impersonators worldwide
- Seven percent of Americans think Elvis is still alive
- The 1952 symphony, "Victory at Sea," written by Richard Rodgers, lasted 13 hours

- Instruments at the Lower Keys Underwater Music Festival include trumpets, harps, guitars, and even trumbones.

TOP FIVE
MUSICAL DEATHS

Five famous musicians who experienced untimely deaths in strange circumstances.

1 "Mama Cass" Elliot of The Mamas and Papas choked to death on a sandwich, 1974

2 Brian Jones of The Rolling Stones drowned in his swimming pool, 1969

3 Terry Kath of Chicago died playing Russian roulette in 1978. His last words were: "Don't worry, it's not loaded"

4 Keith Relf, singer with The Yardbirds, was electrocuted while tuning his guitar, 1976

5 Graham Bond, blues musician, mysteriously fell to his death under a subway train at London's Finsbury Park Station, 1974

Music, including The Beatles' "Yellow Submarine" and extracts from "The Little Mermaid," was piped down through speakers suspended from boats on the surface. Some musical festival participants declare that they have seen fish and other marine creatures also enjoying the concert!

Musical Pigs Farmer Raymond Collier of Hampshire, England, plays classical music to his pigs to boost productivity. He insists that the pigs sleep better after listening to a symphony—unlike his neighbors who have complained about being kept awake at night.

Flight of Fancy In 2003 Bono, lead singer of Irish rock band U2, paid £1,000 ($1,670) to have his favorite hat—a trilby—flown first-class to Italy. He had forgotten to pack it for a charity gig with Luciano Pavarotti.

Death Watch Elvis Presley used to enjoy visiting his local morgue to observe the corpses. He also had a fixation with guns and would use his TV set for target practise.

Early Works Elvis Presley was 21 when he had his first hit. By that age Mozart had written over 250 compositions.

Real Emotion In 1971 while Calgary's KFSM radio station was playing Carole King's "I Feel the Earth Move," the studio collapsed.

Distant Star Pyotr Ilyich Tchaikovsky (1840–93) was awarded a generous annual allowance by wealthy widow Nadezhda von Meck—provided that they never meet. She was convinced that she would be disappointed if ever she met her idol in person.

Rossini Riddle Italian composer Gioacchino Rossini (1792–1868) wrote 53 grand operas before his 11th birthday. How come? He was born on February 29 and his birthdays came only once every four years!

Festival participant Bill Becker flies the American flag as Mel Herlehy strums an underwater guitar.

Biker Beat An "orchestra" of 100 bikers revved up their motorcycles at different intensities at an exhibition in Stockholm in 2000 to perform "Vrooom," a five-minute piece by Swedish composer Staffan Mossenmark. They were conducted by Petter Sundkvist, who waved racetrack flags instead of a baton.

No Sing-along In 2002 Cambodian Prime Minister Hun Sen announced that he was banning all karaoke clubs from the country. He said that any clubs still open would be destroyed by military tanks.

White House Blues President William Howard Taft (1857–1930) was so tone deaf that he couldn't recognize the national anthem. He had to be told when to stand up.

Divers and snorkelers "play" instruments underwater while other divers and snorkelers "listen."

Playing it Cool

The Exhibition of Ice Art takes place at the Nocka Strand in Stockholm. The exhibits, which include musical instruments as well as famous Swedes, are made with water from Sweden's Tome River.

Visitors to the Exhibition of Ice Art protect themselves with warm coats and shoes before they view instruments that are made from 120 tons of clear water ice.

New Wrinkle You're never too old to rock! Twin sisters Kin Narita and Gin Kanie had a hit single in Japan at the age of 99.

Hundreds of 12-ft (4-m) long alphorns are played at the Alpine Horn Festival in Switzerland. Players use a wooden cup-shaped mouthpiece to adjust the sound that emits from the instrument.

Hot Reaction Elizabeth Billington, England's greatest singer of her day, had such a powerful voice that when she sang in Naples in 1794, the Italians accused her of causing the eruption of Mount Vesuvius. She was subsequently driven out of town by the irate residents.

TRAGIC COINCIDENCE

American rock star Duane Allman was killed in a motorbike accident in Macon, Georgia, in 1971. By a macabre coincidence, fellow Allman Brothers member Berry Oakley was killed in another motorbike crash just three blocks away a year later.

In the 1930s Chas Cheer was known as the man with the xylophone head. Tunes could be played on his skull as he formed the notes by opening and closing his mouth.

View from Afar "When Irish Eyes Are Smiling" was written by a German, George Graff, who had never set foot in Ireland in his life.

Memorable Chord French musician Yves Klein composed a "Monotone Symphony," which consists of a single chord held for 20 minutes.

Bagpipe Blunder In the 1960s a Scottish record company released a bagpipe record on which the music was back to front. The error arose after the master tape had been processed from a tape that was accidentally played in reverse. Hundreds of copies were sold before the mistake was spotted.

Don Tranger from Meadville, Pennsylvania, was able to play three trumpets simultaneously, in 1937.

Prophetic Words Lena Gilbert Ford, the lyricist of the song "Keep the Home Fires Burning," died in a fire at her home.

Simon Says Just one man knows whom Carly Simon was singing about in her 1972 hit "You're So Vain." Dick Ebersol, president of NBC Sports, bid $50,000 (£30,000) at a 2003 charity auction for the right to hear the information from Simon herself. The only condition was that he had to swear not to tell anyone else.

Beating the Weather Celebrated drummer Gene Krupa could predict the weather according to the sound of his drums. A dull sound indicated rain while a vibrant tone meant fair weather. In 1944 he claimed never to have made a wrong forecast in 15 years.

Moody Madonna As a teenager Madonna was sacked from a New York Dunkin' Donuts shop for squirting jam at a customer.

Fatal Reversal Known for playing the world's smallest harmonica, Mexican musical maestro Ramon Barrero made an untimely inhalation during a performance at Iguala in 1994 and choked to death on his instrument.

- Ten thousand young Chinese musicians gathered on July 2, 2002 to play six types of percussion instruments in celebration of the fifth anniversary of Hong Kong's handover from Britain to China.

The musical bicycle was invented before radio. Samuel Goss of Chicago fitted piano wires and hammers onto the frame of a bicycle in such a way that different tunes could be played according to the speed of the machine.

CLASSIC STRATEGY

In 2003, Stoke-on-Trent Council in Staffordshire, England, announced that Beethoven's Symphony No. 9 in D Minor would be continuously played in a multi-story parking garage in an attempt to drive away homeless vagrants. It was hoped that the symphony's frequent changes of pitch and time would be so irritating that it would deter the homeless from sleeping there.

Fatal Debut While performing at the New York Metropolitan Opera in 1995, 63-year-old tenor Richard Versalle suffered a fatal heart attack and fell 10 ft (3 m) from a ladder after singing the line "Too bad you can only live so long" from the opening scene of *The Makropulos Case*, a Czech opera about an elixir that ensures eternal youth. Since it was the show's New York premiere, the audience thought it was all part of the plot.

Space Rocks American astronaut Charles Conrad so loved the music of Jerry Lee Lewis that he took a cassette into space on board *Apollo XI.*

Bach to Bach Johann Sebastian Bach came from a family of 62 professional musicians.

The King's Toys Elvis Presley owned 18 television sets, 100 pairs of pants, 21 capes, 8 cars, 7 motorcycles, 3 tractors, 7 golf buggies, 3 mobile homes, and 6 horses!

Determined Diva Romanian folk singer Joan Melu played a two-hour performance, including an interval, at the Capitol Theatre, Melbourne, in 1980, despite the fact that no one turned up to watch her. She even gave an encore!

Short but Sweet An instrumental album recorded by the artist Gadfly lasts for a mere 32 seconds.

Born to be Famous

Not all musicians were born to greatness: Shirley Bassey used to pack chamber pots; Joe Cocker was a gas fitter; Bette Midler worked as a pineapple chunker; Sting had a job as a bus conductor; Cyndi Lauper started out cleaning dog kennels.

Ozzy Osbourne once worked as a slaughterhouse worker.

RUBINI

• *Rubini, the 19th-century king of the Italian tenors and hero of the La Scala Opera House in Milan, once sang a high note with such force that he broke his own collar-bone!*

Ripley's ®

LOUIS ARMSTRONG PORTRAIT
EXHIBIT NO: 22073
CREATED FROM NEARLY 30,000
CRYSTAL RHINESTONES BY KEN BURKITT
OF CANADA

Monsieur Mangetout

When Michel Lotito, a Frenchman from Grenoble, sits down to dinner, the menu might start with a pair of aluminum skis, followed by a supermarket trolley (with a side plate of razor blades) and finish off with a television set, washed down with a few glasses.

Lotito, who goes under the stage name of Monsieur Mangetout (Mr. Eat-All), has made a career out of devouring metal, crockery, and glass without suffering any ill-effects.

Since the age of nine, he has been crunching through coins, cutlery, plates, bicycles (he says the chain is the tastiest part), and even a coffin—empty of course. His finest hour came in Caracas, Venezuela, in 1978 when he began eating a Cessna 150 light aircraft. Taking a few snacks each day, it took him two years to finish it. Lotito attributes his ability to eat and pass these items naturally to the fact that he was born on June 15, 1950—halfway through the middle day of the middle month of the middle year of the 20th century. Puzzled medical experts, however, have a more logical explanation: they found that the lining of his stomach and intestines is twice the thickness of the average human.

Michel Lotito munches his way through an appetizing plate of car parts.

SKIN DEEP

At the 2003 New York International Fringe Festival, Russian dancer Ksenia Vidyaykina did not stop at stripping off her clothes—she then appeared to strip off her skin, too! In a performance called "Trapped," she removed a chiffon toga and then proceeded to peel fake rubber skin from her thighs, complete with dripping red stage blood. She said that the idea was to show the beauty and bravery of stripping off her various layers.

Bukur, a gypsy of Felsendorf, Transylvania, was so overjoyed at the birth of twins that he placed the newborn infants in a huge pot and danced for a full hour with the pot and babies balanced on his head.

Two young sisters from Mongolia, Anu and Mandukhai, show off their stage contortionist tricks in two lockers at Hamburg station in Germany.

Monty Melee A French stage version of *The Full Monty* closed early following a fist-fight between two actors mid-way through a performance. Pierre Cosso, who was taken to hospital with a broken nose, came to blows with Christian Mulot in a row over the levels of noise backstage during his solo spot.

Foot Perfect The Zamalzain, leader of a Basque dance troupe, must leap high in the air and land on a wine glass so lightly that he neither shatters nor spills a single drop of wine.

Chihuahua Cha-Cha Clansko in the Czech Republic stages an annual dance championship with a difference. It is for dogs, which can compete either in solo competitions or with their owners in the couples contest!

The Other RSC Originating in California in 1981, the three-man Reduced Shakespeare Company perform all of the Bard's 37 plays and 154 sonnets—in just 90 minutes.

A Car All at Sea A London Palladium production of the musical *Chitty Chitty Bang Bang,* held in the presence of the Prince of Wales, was abandoned before the interval when the main character—the car—collided on stage with a ship.

FROZEN DANISH
A production of *Hamlet* was staged in a 26-ft (8-m) high ice theater in 2003. The theater in Jukkasjaervi, northern Sweden, is modelled on London's Globe Theatre and so has no roof. Temperatures dipped as low as −24°F (−31°C) during rehearsals.

Pay That Sticks Dancing gypsies in Tirana, Albania, perform with such vitality that onlookers traditionally pay them by placing coins on their foreheads. The dancers sweat so much that the coins stick to their skin.

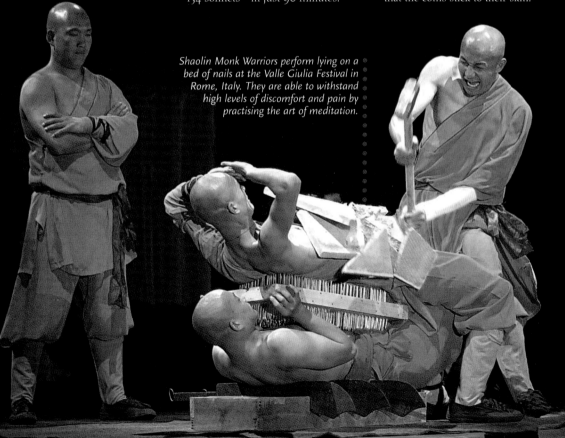

Shaolin Monk Warriors perform lying on a bed of nails at the Valle Giulia Festival in Rome, Italy. They are able to withstand high levels of discomfort and pain by practising the art of meditation.

Jim Tarven was a giant, standing at 7 ft 11 in (2.4 m) tall. He weighed in at 390 lb (176 kg). In contrast, the other half of the double act was Mary Schmidt (in the hat) who was only 3 ft 5 in (1 m) tall and weighed only 84 lb (38 kg). This picture was taken in 1930 when they were part of the Sells-Floto-To-Mix Circus.

Top Marx A production of the *Communist Manifesto* became the surprise hit of the Buenos Aires theater circuit in 2003. The adaptation of the 1848 masterpiece (featuring Karl Marx) drew large audiences when performed by theater company Lucharte at a local bread factory.

Quick Closure Lord Lytton's play, *The Lady Of Lyons,* opened and closed at London's Shaftesbury Theatre on December 26, 1888. After waiting patiently for an hour, the audience was sent home because nobody could raise the safety curtain.

One Good Turn . . . Madame Favart, star of the Opera Comique, Paris, was the first performer to entertain soldiers during wartime. In 1746, at the height of the conflict between France and Austria, she took her entire troupe to the front to amuse French troops. Indeed she proved so popular that the enemy Austrians also asked her to put on a show for their army. So she ended up entertaining both sides!

Theater Buffs Naked ushers were hired by a theater in Berlin to show guests to their seats at the 2003 premiere of *Art Breaks Free* by Christoph Schlingensief.

A giant skeleton representing Death stands in a lake with bony fingers holding open the Book of Life. The stage suspended over the water was the scene for Verdi's opera Un Ball in Maschera at the Bregenz Festival in July 2000. The actors appear dwarfed by this vast set.

Looking Back A secret society of African acrobats, known as the bird men of Guinea, only accept new members if they can swivel their heads a full 180 degrees!

Roaring Success French actor Charles Dullin (1885–1949) had the most dangerous audience imaginable—when he recited poetry in a cage of lions.

No Strings Attached A 1930s Vaudeville contortionist called Brawerman (or "King Brawn") was able to pass his entire body through an unstrung tennis racket.

LIE STILL

Legendary French actress Sarah Bernhardt (1844–1923) used to learn her lines while lying in a coffin. The silk-lined coffin traveled everywhere with her on tour. She also slept in it and used it as a setting for entertaining a series of lovers, among them Napoleon III, novelist Victor Hugo, and the Prince of Wales—the future King Edward VII of England.

Back Seat Sell-out At the Edinburgh Fringe Festival in 1981, the Bogdan Club performed the play *2001* in the back of a Hillman Avenger car. The maximum audience for each performance was four, but safety officials complained because the theater on wheels had neither exit lights nor space between the aisles.

Your Eyes Only Charles Monselet (1825–88), France's leading theater critic for 42 years, never saw a play in his entire lifetime! Instead he always waited in a nearby bar during a premiere where friends later reported their impressions of the play.

Up in Stages An outdoor theater was created annually near Puchheim, Austria, by laying planks across horizontal branches of a tall linden tree. Four stages were set up to create a four-story theater, capable of accommodating 140 actors.

Animal Antics Audiences in ancient Greece were stunned by performers who would pinch part of a goat's neck, cutting off the artery leading to its brain, causing the animal to fall asleep! The goat would then wake when the pressure was released.

The ballerinas of ancient Knossos on the island of Crete used to finish their dance by jumping over a charging wild bull— always leaping between the animal's horns!

Fading Star In a 1787 performance of *Hamlet*, the lead man was so overcome with stage fright on the second night that the play went on without him! Many spectators said they preferred the play without the central character!

THE SMALLEST THEATRE IN THE WORLD

Marcel Steiner performs Macbeth in his own theater—built on a 650cc motorcycle! On another occasion, he performed The Tempest in the parking lot of the Royal Shakespeare Company at Stratford, England, while the RSC was doing a grander version of the same play inside!

Making-up Monsters

Movie make-up techniques have changed—dramatically. For the cult movie *An American Werewolf in London* (U.S. 1981), the pre-digital make-up and body prosthetics were considered ground-breaking in the movie industry at the time.

Traditional make-up was also applied by Rick Baker in films such as the remake of *Planet of the Apes* (U.S. 2001) and *Thriller* by Michael Jackson. But traditional movie make-up could soon be a thing of the past. Hollywood has gone digital. The system employed on *Lord of the Rings: The Two Towers* (U.S./NZ 2002) is called motion capture photography. Actor Andy Serkis would go into a studio wearing a suit with reflective dots all over it, each dot corresponding to a joint in his body, and act out the scene. Twenty-five cameras then fed the information into a computer, which captured his movements and translated them to form the digital version of Gollum. It was this animated Gollum that was seen on screen.

Thanks to advances in digital technology, fantastic visual effects can be achieved without make-up. In the movie Lord of the Rings: The Two Towers, *the character of Gollum was digitally produced to have 300 muscles that actually moved plus 250 different facial expressions. It was part acting, part animation.*

The transition from man to beast in An American Werewolf in London *took Oscar-winning make-up artist Rick Baker ten hours a day to complete.*

Tom Hanks is related to Abraham Lincoln. He is a direct descendant of Nancy Hanks, Lincoln's mother.

ACTORS' FIRST JOBS

- Warren Beatty—rat-catcher
- Sylvester Stallone—lion-cage cleaner
- Errol Flynn—sheep-castrator
- Sean Connery—polisher for coffin-maker
- Keanu Reeves—manager of a pasta shop in Toronto
- Burt Lancaster—lingerie salesman
- Michelle Pfeiffer—checkout girl at a grocery store
- Alan Ladd—hot-dog seller
- Kirk Douglas—window-cleaner
- Jayne Mansfield—saucepan seller

Siamese Twin At birth, American actor Andy Garcia, had a twin about the size of a small ball joined to his left shoulder. The twin was surgically removed but died soon afterward.

Agent Who? At the age of ten, Leonardo DiCaprio was advised by his agent to change his name to a more American-friendly Lenny Williams.

Ill Wind Vivien Leigh hated kissing Clark Gable on *Gone With The Wind* (U.S. 1939) because she said he had terrible breath.

Pampered Pooch It's a dog's life. When Ava Gardner died in 1990, she left her pet corgi Morgan a monthly income plus his own limo and maid.

Sticky Drain The blood used for the shower scene in Alfred Hitchcock's 1960 horror movie *Psycho* (U.S. 1960) was really chocolate syrup. The scene took seven days to shoot.

Like No Udder In early Clarabelle Cow cartoons, the cow's udder was always discreetly draped by an apron for fear of upsetting those with high morals.

Silver Lining Mel Gibson won his leading role in the movie *Mad Max* (Aus 1979) because the producers were looking for someone who looked weary, beaten, and scarred. The night before his screen test, Gibson had been attacked by three drunks.

Judy's Roots Judy Garland was a descendant of former U.S. President Ulysses S. Grant.

Extra "Extras"
Some movie-makers go to extreme lengths to achieve a realistic scene. In Richard Attenborough's movie *Gandhi*, (U.K. 1982) more extras appeared on screen than in any previous historical epic. Other movie-makers have been known to draft in regiments, even whole armies, to take part in a scene, as in the Nazi-made epic, *Kolberg* (Ger 1947).

On the set of Gandhi (U.K. 1982), the director employed 300,000 extras to play mourners in the opening funeral scene.

Kate's Honey Kate Winslet, star of *Titanic* (U.S. 1997), first appeared on screen dancing with the Honey Monster in a TV commercial for Sugar Puffs breakfast cereal.

Movie Mania In India every day more than 15 million Indians go to the movies.

Chaplinesque Charlie Chaplin once came third in a Charlie Chaplin lookalike contest.

No Hopers While at school, the now successful actors Gene Hackman, Dustin Hoffman, and Robin Williams were voted "Least Likely to Succeed" by their classmates.

Eyes Wide Shut Screen tough guy Edward G. Robinson hated playing hoodlum roles. In fact, the sound of gunfire made him squint so badly that his eyelids had to be taped open.

Spiderman In 1993 a newly discovered species of spider was named *Calponia harrisonfordi* in honor of Hollywood star Harrison Ford's movie role fear of arachnids.

Bela Lugosi (1882–1956) was the vampire who couldn't stand the sight of blood. Famed for his blood-thirsty portrayal of Count Dracula in movies, Lugosi often fainted at the sight of real blood.

LIMELIGHT

A North Wales lighthouse with room for a 12-strong audience staged a movie premiere in 2003. South Stack lighthouse on Anglesey Island showed a 15-minute film by Elaine Townson called *The Birds and a Suitcase* (U.K. 2002). Not the easiest venue to reach, the audience had to climb down more than 400 steps to get to the remote cinema.

King-sized Waste For the remake of *King Kong* (U.S. 1976), producers ordered the construction of a 40-ft (12-m) high, 13,000-lb (5,896-kg), electronically controlled robot with a 20-ft (6-m) arm span covered with two tons of horse hair to simulate fur. Yet the expensive creation appeared for only ten seconds of the movie, the majority of which featured an actor in a gorilla suit playing on miniature sets!

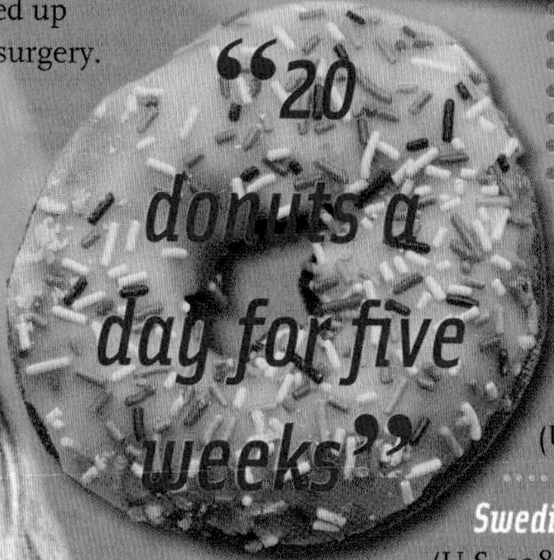

Movie Marathon Thai film buffs watched 36 films in two-and-a-half days in 2003, beating an American record set two years earlier. The 17-person group watched films for 64 hr 58 minutes as part of the Bangkok International Film Festival. They took a 15-minute break after every third film.

Unbuttoned Alfred Hitchcock didn't have a belly button. It disappeared when he was stitched up following surgery.

"20 donuts a day for five weeks"

Renée Zellweger had to go from a size 6 to a size 14 for her starring role in Bridget Jones: The Edge of Reason (U.S. 2004).

Sole Sister Reese Witherspoon had 63 pairs of shoes specially made for her movie *Legally Blonde 2* (U.S. 2003).

Swedish Ban The family film *E.T.* (U.S. 1982) was banned in Sweden for youngsters under eleven because of fears that it showed parents being hostile to their children.

Good Old Mom When Cary Grant played the son of Jessie Royce Landis in *North by Northwest* (U.S. 1959), he was 55 and she was 54!

Renée Zellweger, seen here in Bridget Jones's Diary (U.S. 2001), ate 20 donuts a day for five weeks to pile on 14 lb (6.5 kg) for the sequel, Bridget Jones: The Edge of Reason (U.S. 2004). Her diet also included a burger with large fries, savoury scones with gravy, and a high-fat milkshake—all for breakfast!

More than 1,600 pairs of latex ears and feet were used during the filming of The Lord of the Rings: The Two Towers, (U.S./NZ 2002) each cooked in a special oven.

TOP FIVE
HOLLYWOOD ACTRESSES
(based on earnings in 2002)

1 **Julia Roberts** $20.3m (£12m) per film

2 **Cameron Diaz** $20m (£11m) per film

3 **Drew Barrymore** $15.6m (£7m) per film

4 **Jodie Foster** $15.6m (£7m) per film

5 **Reese Witherspoon** $15.6m (£7m) per film

Scary Cartoon Mickey Mouse was banned in Romania in 1935 because the authorities thought a 10-ft (3-m) high rodent on screen was likely to scare the nation's children.

Mouse Mail Mickey Mouse received 800,000 fan letters a year.

Presidential Rejection A movie script written by President Franklin D. Roosevelt about *Old Ironsides*, one of the United States' most famous warships, was rejected by Hollywood.

Dad's Watching Actress Evelyn Venable, voice of the Blue Fairy in *Pinocchio*, (U.S. 1940) was forbidden to kiss on screen—upon the orders of her father.

Horse Play Mack Sennett, producer of *The Keystone Cops*, began his career playing the hind legs of a stage horse!

Straight Man Buster Keaton's contract with MGM in the 1920s prevented him from smiling on screen.

Language, Please! Clara Bow (1905–65) had it written into her contract with Paramount that none of the crew would use profane language in her presence. In return she was offered a $500,000 (£300,000) bonus if she remained free of scandal. She failed to collect.

Duck Out Donald Duck was once banned in Finland because he doesn't wear pants!

Flawed Stars
Things may appear perfect in the movie world but they are not always what they seem: Demi Moore was born cross-eyed; Clark Gable is listed on his birth certificate as a girl; the Oscars were made of wood during World War II —to conserve metal; and Johnny Depp has a phobia about clowns.

Clint Eastwood is allergic to horses.

Index

Jacket (b/l) Sipa/Rex Features

8 (b) Layne Kennedy/CORBIS; 9 (b) Tony Kyriacou/REX; 11(t) Gideon
Mendel/CORBIS; 13 (t/l) Ashley Gilbertson/AFP/GETTYIMAGE, (t/r) Ulrich
Perrey/AFP/GETTYIMAGE, (b) Robyn Beck/AFP/GETTYIMAGE; 14 (b) Robyn
Beck/AFP/GETTYIMAGE; 15 (t/r) AFP/GETTYIMAGE, (b) Joern
Pollex/AFP/GETTYIMAGE; 16 (t) James Leynse/CORBIS, (b) Frederic J.
Brown/AFP/GETTYIMAGE; 17 (t/r) Sourav/AFP/GETTYIMAGE; 18 (b) Courtesy
of Warner; 20 (l) Idranil Mukherjee/AFP/GETTYIMAGE; 21 (t) Sipa Press /REX;
22 (b) Bill Keogh/AFP/GETTYIMAGE; 23 (t) Bill Keogh/AFP/GETTYIMAGE,
(b) Bill Keogh/AFP/GETTYIMAGE; 24 (t) Sven Nackstrand/AFP/GETTYIMAGE,
(b) Stefan Puchner/AFP/GETTYIMAGE; 25 (b/r) Peter Parks/AFP/GETTYIMAGE;
26 (t/r) Pictorial Press Ltd; 27 (t) Nils Jorgensen/REX; 28 (t) Carsten
Rehder/AFP/GETTYIMAGE, (b) Maria Laura/REX; 29 (b) Moma/AFP/
GETTYIMAGE; 30 (b/l) James Fraser/REX; 31 (t/r) Courtesy of Polygram,
(c/r) Courtesy of Polygram, (b) Entertainmant/New Line; 32 (t/l) Pictorial Press
Ltd, (t/r) Pictorial Press Ltd, (b) Columbia/Goldcrest; 33 (c) Pictorial Press Ltd;
34 (t/r) Pictorial Press Ltd, (c) Universal/Miramax, (b/l) Entertainment/New Line;
35 (t/l) Entertainment/New Line, (b) Pictorial Press Ltd.

All other photos are from Corel, MKP archives, PhotoDisc,
Digital Vision and Ripley's Entertainment Inc.

Now Available!

More than **250** pages of all-new **bizarre** and **intriguing** facts, images, features, interviews, and stories presenting a host of **extraordinary** people, places, and creatures that will **stretch** your credulity and imagination to its limits!